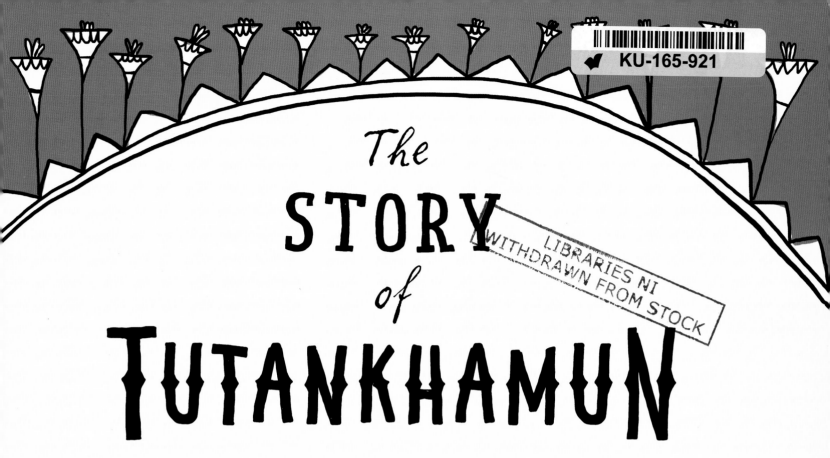

The STORY of TUTANKHAMUN

"The history of Egypt literally comes out of the ground piece by piece..." PROFESSOR JOANN FLETCHER

PATRICIA CLEVELAND-PECK

Illustrated by ISABEL GREENBERG

BLOOMSBURY
LONDON OXFORD NEW YORK NEW DELHI SYDNEY

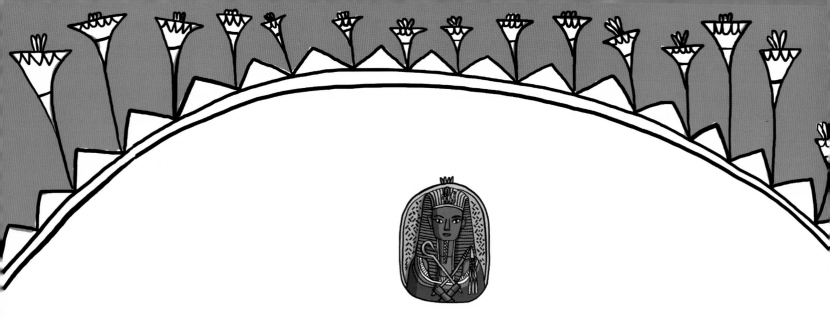

If you'd like to find out more about the ancient Egyptians, lots of museums have brilliant exhibitions, including: The British Museum (London, UK), The Metropolitan Museum of Art (New York, USA), The Egyptian Museum (Cairo, Egypt).

Bloomsbury Children's Books
An imprint of Bloomsbury Publishing Plc

50 Bedford Square
London
WC1B 3DP
UK

www.bloomsbury.com

BLOOMSBURY and the Diana logo are trademarks of Bloomsbury Publishing Plc

First published in Great Britain 2017

A catalogue record for this book is available from the British Library.

Library of Congress Cataloguing-in-Publication data has been applied for.

ISBN 978 1 4088 7678 7

2 4 6 8 10 9 7 5 3 1

Printed and bound in China by Leo Paper Products, Heshan, Guangdong

MIX
Paper from
responsible sources
FSC® C020056

To find out more about our authors and books visit www.bloomsbury.com.
Here you will find extracts, author interviews, details of forthcoming events
and the option to sign up for our newsletters.

OUR STORY BEGINS

This is the story of Tutankhamun, one of the most famous kings from throughout history. Everything we know about him, and the time he lived in, comes from the archaeological discoveries of ancient Egyptian tombs, uncovered thousands of years after his death.

Tombs are still being found today and modern technology has made it possible for us to re-examine evidence and come to new and sometimes startling conclusions. Read on to uncover the incredible facts that have been discovered so far . . .

PART ONE

··· 6 ···

PART TWO

··· 18 ···

PART THREE

··· 61 ···

IN THIS BOOK YOU WILL MEET

'I am the Pharaoh Tutankhamun. Like all pharaohs I have five names'

'I am Ankhesenamun, Great Royal Wife and half-sister of Tutankhamun'

'I am King Akhenaten, father of both Ankhesenamun and Tutankhamun'

'I am Queen Nefertiti, Great Royal Wife of King Akhenaten, mother of Ankhesenamun and mother-in-law of Tutankhamun'

'I am Tiye, mother of King Akhenaten and grandmother of Tutankhamun'

'I am Ay, Vizier (high official), and brother of Tiye'

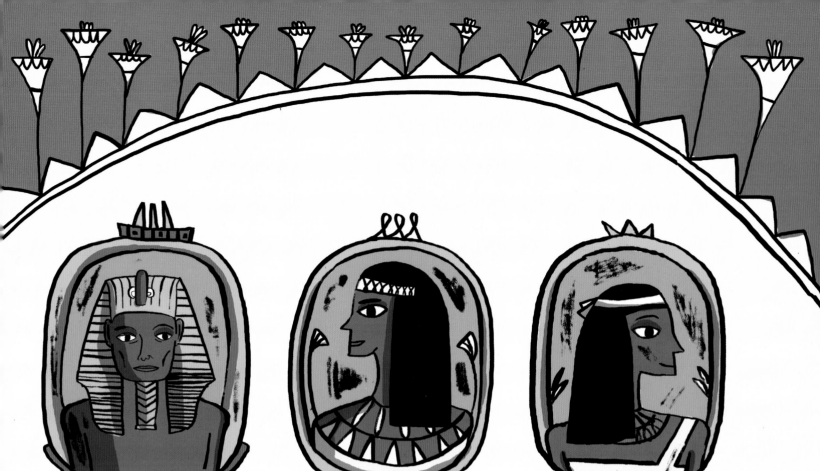

'I am Horemheb, general of the Egyptian army'

'I am Tia, wet nurse to My Lady Ankhesenamun'

'I am Maia, wet nurse to His Highness, Tutankhamun'

And introducing our archaeologists and adventurers...

Howard Carter

Theodore Davis

Earl of Carnarvon

Lady Evelyn

PART ONE

The boy king is dead!
The falcon is flown to heaven . . .

Tutankhamun was born at a time of change. His grandfather, Amenhotep, had governed with the influential Queen Tiye at his side and together they ruled a great empire. When Amenhotep died, Tutankhamun's father, King Akhenaten, became Pharaoh. At this time Egypt was a rich and powerful country, however, by the end of Akhenaten's reign, almost everything was lost.

Akhenaten married the beautiful Queen Nefertiti and they had six cherished daughters together. Akhenaten loved his family dearly. We know this because archaeologists have uncovered pictures of him kissing and hugging his children. To create pictures like these was very unusual at the time.

ATEN

HORUS

ANUBIS

RA

SET

ISIS

THOTH

OSIRIS

HATHOR

King Akhenaten made some unpopular religious changes during his reign. It was these changes that would eventually lead to his downfall. Prior to his reign the Egyptians worshipped many gods – the god Amun was one of the most important. However, Akhenaten became obsessed with one god – Aten – the sun disc. He rejected the old gods and closed their temples, which upset a lot of people, especially the priests. He moved the court to a new palace-city called Akhetaten, which he had designed himself.

Akhenaten also made everyone in the family change their names so that they ended with 'aten', which means 'pleasing to Aten'. Akhenaten's full name had been Amenhotep IV, so he then became Akhenaten. When a little boy was born to one of Akhenaten's lesser wives (pharaohs often had lots of wives), he was called Tutankhaten. It was this boy who would go on to succeed his father and become the famous Tutankhamun.

Not much is known about Tutankhamun's mother. However, Tutankhamun's grandmother, Queen Tiye, probably played an important part in his life: a lock of her red hair, which he had kept in a tiny coffin-shaped box, was found in his tomb. Royal children were brought up by wet nurses, who were often members of court families. Nefertiti's wet nurse had married a very important official named Ay, who would later play a monumental role in Tutankhamun's life. Tutankhamun's own wet nurse was called Maia and the bond between them must have been strong because later he had an elaborate tomb made for her.

As a boy Tutankhamun ran about naked. His hair was shaved except for one long tuft on the right, which was plaited. The young prince played games like tug of war and 'jumping the goose' (a sort of 'leapfrog'), and owned balls and toys such as a pull-along cat whose mouth opened as it moved. Live pets such as cats, kittens, monkeys and birds like hoopoes were very popular with children too. The princesses, Tutankhamun's half-sisters, even kept pet gazelles.

As well as lots of toys and pets, the royal family had lavish meals and parties and owned magnificent barges, which they used for floating picnics.

Princes in ancient Egypt were instructed in reading, writing and arithmetic. Sporting activities were also important; shooting, rowing, swimming and handling horses and chariots were all part of a royal prince's education.

Meanwhile, the state of Egypt was going from bad to worse. King Akhenaten did not want to leave his palace-city, so it is believed that Queen Nefertiti and her eldest daughter, Princess Meritaten, left Akhetaten to try and maintain royal power (possibly in Luxor or Memphis). However, after their departure from Akhetaten, nothing was heard of either of them. It has been suggested that Nefertiti governed herself for a while using the male name of Smenkhkare, but no one knows for sure.

What is certain is that within a short time all members of the royal family were dead, except for the young Tutankhamun. The country's finances were low and Egypt's rivals, the Hittites, had extended their territory. This is when Tutankhamun, a boy of around nine years old, became king. Egypt hailed their new leader:

Due to Tutankhamun's young age it was decided that Vizier Ay, who had always been close to the family (and had married Nefertiti's wet nurse), would act as his guardian.

Soon after this, another important decision was made on Tutankhamun's behalf: that he should marry... and his half-sister Ankhesenamun was chosen to be his Great Royal Wife.

AMUN

It was then announced that the new pharaoh intended to restore the old gods. It is unlikely that this decision was made by Tutankhamun, but was probably another decision made on his behalf. Nevertheless, Aten the sun disc was no longer seen as the most powerful god, and Amun, who was traditionally a very powerful god, was worshipped again. The palace at Akhetaten was abandoned and the court returned to their traditional palace in Thebes. Now that the old gods, and especially Amun, were back in favour, everyone had to change their names again, this time replacing 'aten' with 'amun'. And so Prince Tutankhaten became King Tutankhamun.

Tutankhamun and Ankhesenamun had known each other almost all of their lives and when they married they seemed to be a loving couple. However, tragedy may have clouded their young marriage when they lost not one, but both of their babies.

It is unlikely that Tutankhamun had much say in governmental matters or the appointment of gods during his reign. But after the unrest of King Akhenaten's rule, it was extremely important to win back the support of the public and have a stable leader. This task fell to Vizier Ay, because of his influence as Tutankhamun's guardian.

THEBES

However, even Vizier Ay had a rival in the ambitious Commander-in-Chief of the Army, General Horemheb. Horemheb had risen to a position of power by reasserting Egyptian authority abroad. After Tutankhamun's rule, both Ay and Horemheb would go on to become pharaohs.

It is thought that Tutankhamun did not take part in any military campaigns himself: possibly because of his poor health. Despite his poor health, no one was prepared for the sudden shock of his death. Records suggest that he was just 18 or 19 years old when he died and to this day, no one knows for certain what caused his death. The mystery of Tutankhamun's short life would continue to be unravelled long after his time.

Countless theories of how he died have been discussed over the years. Perhaps he was murdered? Both Ay and Horemheb had something to gain if he was out of the way. Or perhaps he died of natural causes – scientists now know that he had malaria. But the biggest mystery that puzzled historians and archaeologists for many years was: where was Tutankhamun's tomb?

MUMMIFICATION

All ancient Egyptians, including pharaohs, were mummified when they died. The process of mummification was extremely important to the ancient Egyptians, who paid vast amounts of money to have their bodies properly preserved. It was a complex procedure and took 70 days to complete! It was conducted by a priest wearing the jackal-headed mask of Anubis, god of the dead. Anubis was responsible for conducting the dead through the underworld.

Mummification was a messy and unpleasant process and so was done well away from other people.

To begin with, the body was taken to a tent known as the Place of Purification.

The body was washed with sweet-smelling wine and Nile water. Then a cut was made in the left side of the body and the liver, lungs, intestines and stomach were removed. They were washed and packed in a type of salt called 'natron' to dry out.

They were then placed in special jars called canopic jars.
The heart was not removed during this process because it, rather then the brain, was believed to be the centre of man's intelligence and so would be needed in the afterlife.

Next, the brain was removed. A long hook was used to smash it up and the bits were then pulled out through the nose. The body was covered with natron to dry it out.

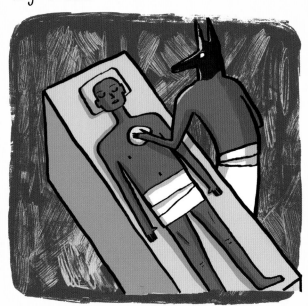

After 40 days the body was washed again, then covered with oils to keep it supple.

It was then stuffed with dry material, such as leaves, to reshape it. The cut in the left side of the body was sewn up and sealed with resin.

Finally, the body was wrapped up, using hundreds of yards of linen. First the head and neck, then the fingers and toes, and then the arms and legs. Amulets were placed between each layer to keep the body safe.

During this process the Priest read a spell to ward off evil. The arms and legs were tied together, and papyrus with spells from the Book of the Dead (this contains magic spells to help the deceased journey to the afterlife) were placed between the hands. More bindings were wrapped over the body and liquid resin was used to glue them together.

Now the senses enjoyed in life would function in the afterlife, so the deceased could speak, hear, see and eat.

Religious rituals were performed at the funeral. The most important of these was the 'Opening the Mouth' ritual, during which various parts of the body were symbolically touched to 'open' them.

A pharaoh's funeral procession would journey from his palace to the tomb on the West Bank. The priests would burn incense and shake sistra (rattle-like musical instruments) as they walked.

For years, historians have been trying to uncover whose tomb might have been used instead.

Ancient Egyptians were not afraid of death, but they wanted life to continue into the afterlife, so after someone had died there was a rush to furnish the tomb with all that would be needed. But Tutankhamun's death was so sudden that his intended tomb was not ready.

PART TWO

Howard Carter: the discovery of the boy king

More than 3,000 years after the burial of Tutankhamun, another boy was born in England – Howard Carter. Like Tutankhamun, Carter was often ill as a child, but would live to play a huge part in Tutankhamun's story.

Carter's father was an artist and Carter grew up with 10 brothers and sisters. As his health was poor he didn't go to school but instead was taught at home by his aunties. Later, when he mixed with people from well-known schools and universities, he felt uncomfortable and out of place. As a result, he sometimes behaved in a grumpy, stubborn way, which could get him into trouble. From a young age

Carter's father taught him to draw and paint. Carter became an extremely talented artist and this, coupled with his determination and intelligence, led him to secure a job at the age of just 17 as a 'tracer' in Egypt, drawing details of tomb scenes.

He loved Egypt from the first moment he set foot there and soon wanted to excavate tombs himself. He displayed an incredible talent at excavation and before long was made 'Inspector General of Monuments of Upper Egypt'. This meant that he worked in the famous Valley of the Kings: the burial place of many pharaohs.

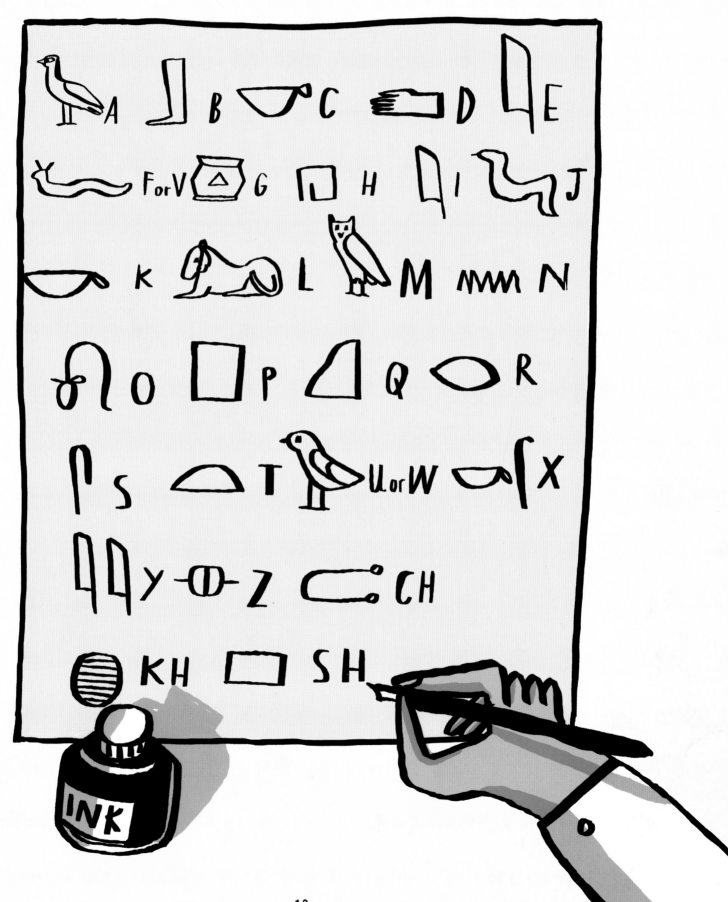

Anyone who wanted to dig in the Valley of the Kings had to buy a permit, known as a 'concession', from the Egyptian government. These were expensive but if the tomb had been robbed in the past (and most of them had), the permit owner might be allowed to keep some of the treasure. Because tombs had been looted, throughout time, it was hard to know exactly what they contained.

For a while Carter worked with an American archaeologist, Theodore Davis, who held the concession for the Valley of the Kings. However, the pair didn't get on because Davis was seen as a sloppy, careless archaeologist and Carter was just the opposite. During their time working together, Carter discovered that Davis was searching for Tutankhamun's tomb (which he came very close to finding). This made Carter want to find it himself – but he had very little information to go on.

Many references to the 18th dynasty had been removed by General Horemheb when he eventually became pharaoh. Horemheb hated Ay and completely destroyed sites and monuments so it was as if Ay, and also Akhenaten and Tutankhamun, never existed.

ALEXANDRIA

GIZA
SAQQARA
HELIOPOLIS
CAIRO

MEMPHIS

RED SEA

AKHETATEN

VALLEY OF
THE KINGS

KARNAK
LUXOR
THEBES

ASWAN

ANCIENT EGYPT

ABU SIMBEL

After working with Davis, Carter moved to a new job at Saqqara, the ancient cemetery of the city of Memphis. However, an unfortunate incident along with Carter's stubborn streak nearly cost him his career. A group of rowdy French tourists wanted to visit the burial place of the sacred Apis bulls. Carter was in charge of the site and the tourists became angry when they were told they needed tickets to enter. Some pushed in without paying and charged into the site. However, it was dark inside and the tourists couldn't see anything. They rushed back out again and those who had paid asked for their money back. Carter refused, told them to leave and a scuffle broke out. The French tourists complained and Carter was advised to apologise but he said he would rather resign – which he did.

Having lost his job, Carter was forced to sell his own paintings of Egypt to tourists for money. He also sold objects taken from tombs. This would certainly not be allowed today but at the time it was considered acceptable.

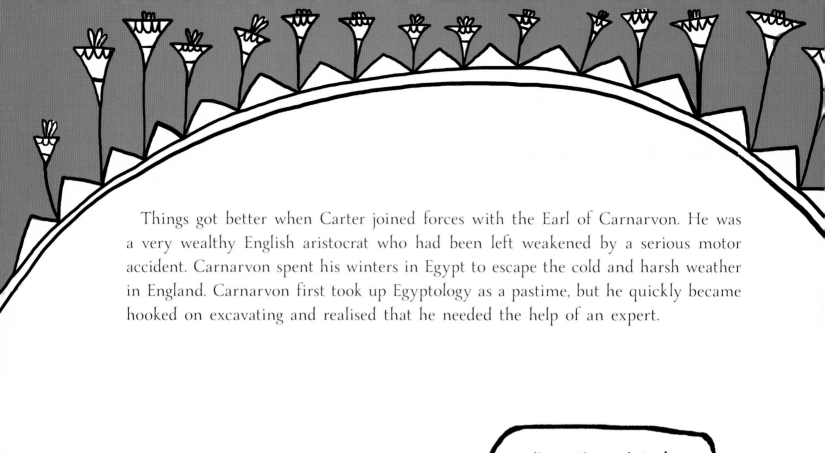

Things got better when Carter joined forces with the Earl of Carnarvon. He was a very wealthy English aristocrat who had been left weakened by a serious motor accident. Carnarvon spent his winters in Egypt to escape the cold and harsh weather in England. Carnarvon first took up Egyptology as a pastime, but he quickly became hooked on excavating and realised that he needed the help of an expert.

'I am Howard Carter; it is my knowledge and skill which resulted in the discovery of the tomb of Tutankhamun.'

Carnarvon met Carter and they got on well. They both wanted to work in the Valley of the Kings where Carter was itching to search for Tutankhamun's tomb. However, he couldn't, as Davis still owned the concession. Carter became even more impatient when he learned that Davis had found a blue funeral cup bearing Tutankhamun's name.

'I am George Edward Stanhope Molyneux Herbert, 5th Earl of Carnarvon, titled Lord Porchester (until 1890), known as Porch to my family — see, I've as many names as any pharaoh! It is my money which paid for the excavation which resulted in the discovery of the tomb of Tutankhamun.'

Finally in 1914, Davis, now old and ill, gave up his concession and Carnarvon was able to buy it. The outbreak of World War One slowed things down but over the next few years Carter began his search for Tutankhamun's tomb, clearing the Valley down to bedrock using a Decauville hand-operated railway.

The war ended but costs had mounted and with nothing to show after almost ten years, Carnarvon told Carter he couldn't pay for any more excavation. Carter offered to finance one more season himself. Faced with Carter's determination, the Earl gave in and footed the bill for one last dig.

THE DISCOVERY

On the 4th November 1922, after three days of digging near to where Davis had found the blue funeral cup, the top of a sunken staircase was discovered. Carter was very excited.

The steps were quickly cleared and they found a blocked doorway covered with blurry oval seals. Was the tomb for which he had searched for so many years behind this door?

He desperately wanted to open it, but instead sent a telegram to Carnarvon who was in England at the time, so that he too could be there when it was opened.

TO: LORD CARNARVON
FROM: HOWARD CARTER
AT LAST HAVE MADE
WONDERFUL DISCOVERY
IN VALLEY; A
MAGNIFICENT TOMB
WITH SEALS INTACT;
HAVE RE-COVERED SAME
FOR YOUR ARRIVAL;
CONGRATULATIONS.

Carnarvon arrived in Egypt with his daughter Lady Evelyn on 23rd November. They were thrilled when they saw that some of the seals on the door clearly stated the name, Tut.ankh.Amen. However, they were disappointed to see that the door had previously been opened and reclosed – presumably by tomb raiders. Beyond the door they saw a sloping corridor filled to the ceiling with stone chippings. Carter had these chippings removed, which revealed a second doorway.

THE OPENING OF THE TOMB

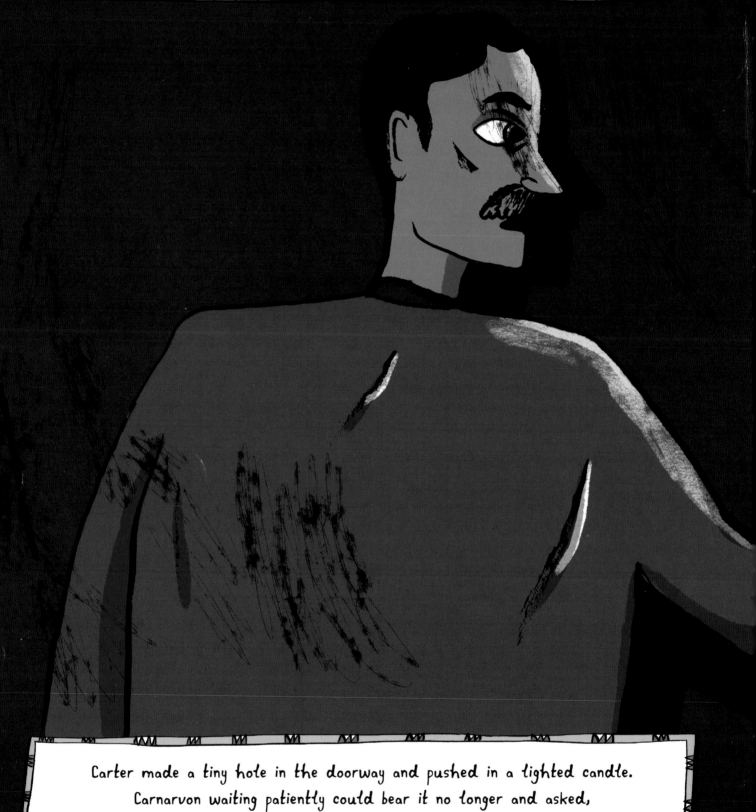

Carter made a tiny hole in the doorway and pushed in a lighted candle. Carnarvon waiting patiently could bear it no longer and asked, 'Can you see anything?'

'Yes,' Carter answered simply. 'Wonderful things.'
They made the hole bigger and scrambled down into what was to be called The Antechamber. By the flickering light of the candle, shadows danced on the walls showing hundreds of things; gold-covered couches in the shape of giant animals, chariots, statues of the king, caskets, vases, black shrines and one with a gold snake peeking out, an alabaster cup, bouquets of flowers, beds, chairs, boxes . . .

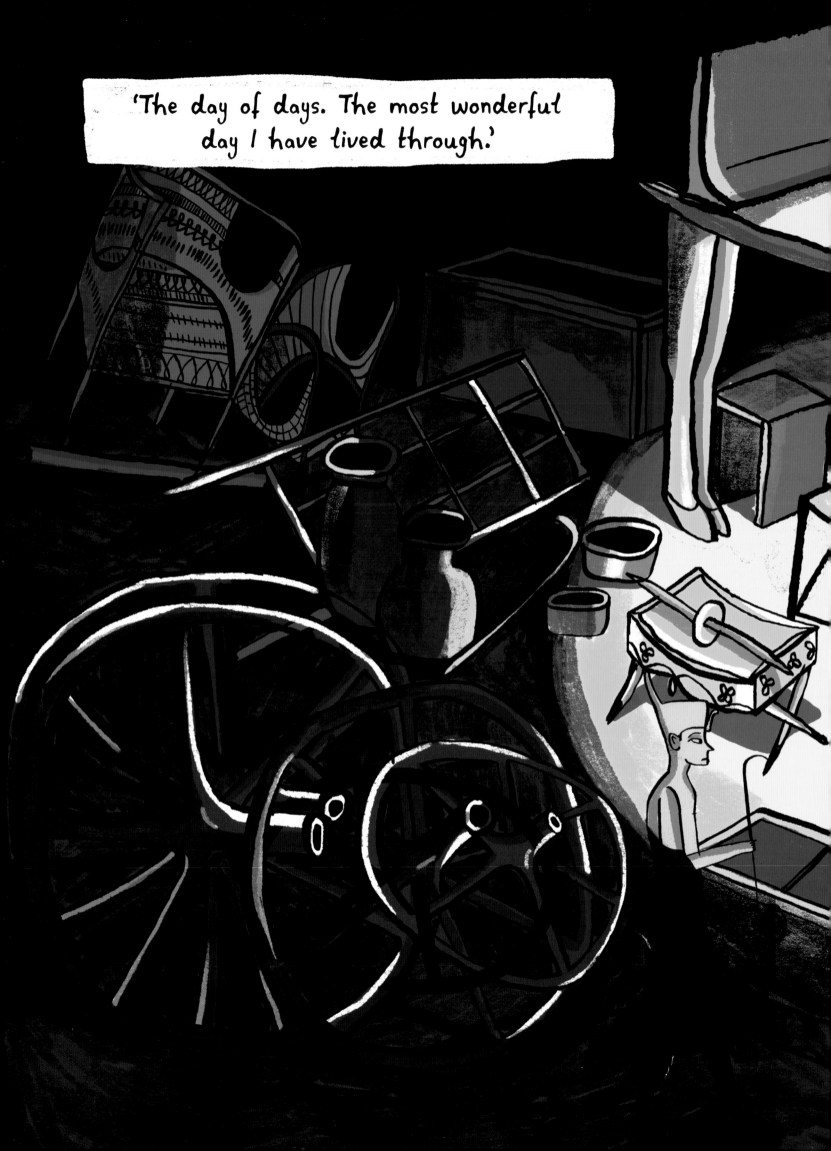

They returned the next day with another member of the team, Pecky Callender, who installed electric lights, which made the scene even more dazzling. The three men and Lady Evelyn could now see the entrance to another room and between two black wooden 'guardian' statues, another sealed door leading to a third chamber. They made a small hole at the bottom of this sealed door and first Carter, then Carnarvon, then Lady Evelyn wriggled through.

This was it, the Burial Chamber!
Carter could hardly believe it.

Knowing how important security was, Carter ordered a large steel gate from Cairo and kept the tomb guarded until it arrived. He then quickly began contacting experts in order to put together a full team to deal with the task of clearing the tomb.

Meanwhile, the hole through which they had wriggled was quietly resealed (as though it had not yet been opened), and preparations for a formal opening of the tomb began. For this, 20 dignitaries were seated in the now empty Antechamber. Both Carnarvon and Carter made speeches and the doorway was opened as if for the first time.

The door opened onto what appeared to be a wall of solid gold – it was really the side of the outer shrine, or container, within which the stone sarcophagus and a series of coffins were to be found. The shrine almost filled the entire room, and scattered on the floor were various objects which had probably been dropped by the robbers: wine jars, an animal skin full of solution for washing the body, and a funeral bouquet.

THE BURIAL CHAMBER

The walls of the Burial Chamber were the only decorated walls in the whole of Tutankhamun's tomb.

What was depicted was of great interest, especially a scene on the north wall, which showed the 'Opening of the Mouth' ceremony.

This painting was unusual because Ay was performing the ceremony, and he was already wearing the crown of the new pharaoh. By tradition, the new king could not be crowned until the last one was sealed in his tomb.

Carter also noticed that the paintings had been finished hastily. Carter would continue to find more and more evidence that suggested that this has been a very rushed burial. The mysteries of Tutankhamun's death looked set to continue.

The shrine not only took up most of the space within the chamber, but it was also very difficult to open. In the end a wall had to be taken down!

Carter wrote: "we bumped our heads, nipped our fingers . . . and had to squeeze in and out like weasels".

As the excavation continued, Carter and his team discovered four shrines, one within the other, decorated with images of gods and magical texts, before the golden stone sarcophagus at the centre.

It was intact! No tomb robber had succeeded in getting this far.

So began the important job of photographing, drawing and recording. Carter was very thorough. Every object was given a number and a note made of where it was found. Items were then put in boxes and taken by the Decauville Railway to Cairo.

The discovery was now world news and an international craze for anything Egyptian broke out, bringing hordes of tourists to the Valley of the Kings. Worried and exhausted, Carter and Carnarvon began to bicker.

On 28th February, Carnarvon left to take a short break in Aswan.
There he was bitten on the cheek by a mosquito and later, while shaving,
he cut the bite which became infected. He had never been strong and
the infection led to blood poisoning and pneumonia.

On 5th April he died.
He never saw the mask of the boy king.

THE CURSE

Just two weeks before this, a writer of popular romantic novels, Marie Corelli, had written, "The most dire punishment follows any rash intruder into a sealed tomb". From this the rumour of 'The Curse of Tutankhamun's Tomb' gathered momentum. Gossip spread quickly and rumours of the curse began to emerge:

At the moment of Carnarvon's death the lights went out all over Cairo.

At the same time his terrier in England howled and dropped dead.

His pet canary was swallowed by a cobra — a cobra was depicted on the Pharaoh's brow.

Later his younger brother Aubrey died suddenly.

An Egyptian (Prince Ali Kamel Fahmy Bey) was shot by his wife at the London Savoy Hotel after viewing the tomb.

An American magnate (George Jay Gould) died of a cold caught at the tomb.

Arthur Mace, one of the team, died before the tomb had been cleared.

A French Egyptologist (Georges Bénédite) died from a fall after seeing the tomb.

There was a lesion on the face of the mummy in the same place as Carnarvon's mosquito bite.

In fact these rumours were all completely ridiculous - the lights often went out all over Cairo, and most of the team lived until a ripe old age.

THE SARCOPHAGUS

eanwhile, work under Carter's command continued. The fact that the sarcophagus had been found was a huge relief. However, the heavy stone lid – which had clearly not been made for this particular sarcophagus – had to be winched up. This sarcophagus lid had been broken and hastily repaired before the burial: this did not look like the carefully planned tomb of a king.

Inside the sarcophagus were three magnificently-decorated, human-shaped coffins nestling one within the other, with linen shrouds between them. Each bore a painted facial mask. However, the second mask was different from the first and the third. If they had all been made for Tutankhamun they would probably have matched. Was this more evidence that Tutankhamun had not been the intended owner of the Burial Chamber, and had been buried in a hurry?

The third coffin was made of pure gold (the weight of which took eight men to lift!) However, there was a problem. It appeared that a quantity of thick, black liquid had been poured into this coffin and it had done a considerable amount of damage. Was this another sign that the mummification had been rushed?

Even with this unfortunate damage, what was revealed was stunning. Shining out of the darkness they saw Tutankhamun's brilliant gold portrait mask, with kohl-rimmed eyes of quartz and obsidian. A vulture and a cobra reared up against his brow, with the cobra poised ready to spit poison at Tutankhamun's enemies. Inscribed on the back of the mask was a spell from the Book of the Dead. Tutankhamun also wore a beard of gold and a broad collar, and his hands were covered with sheet gold.

A vulture and a cobra reared up against his brow, with the cobra poised ready to spit poison at Tutankhamun's enemies.

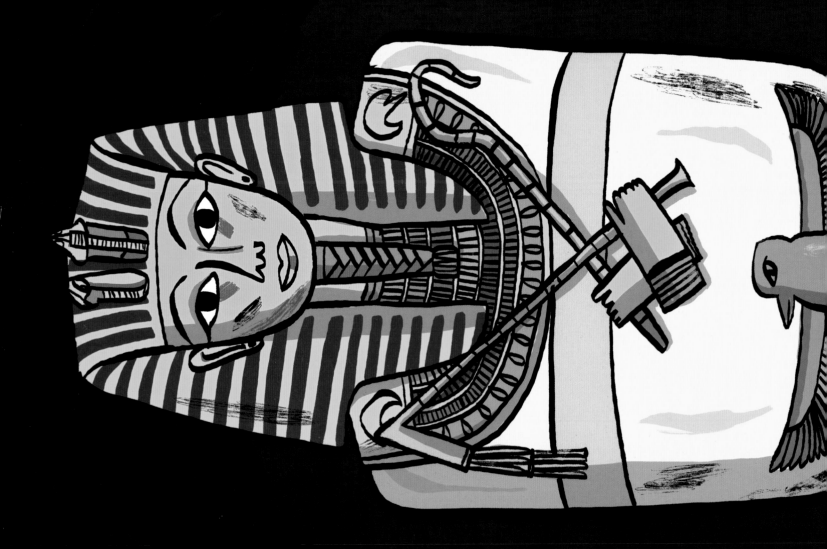

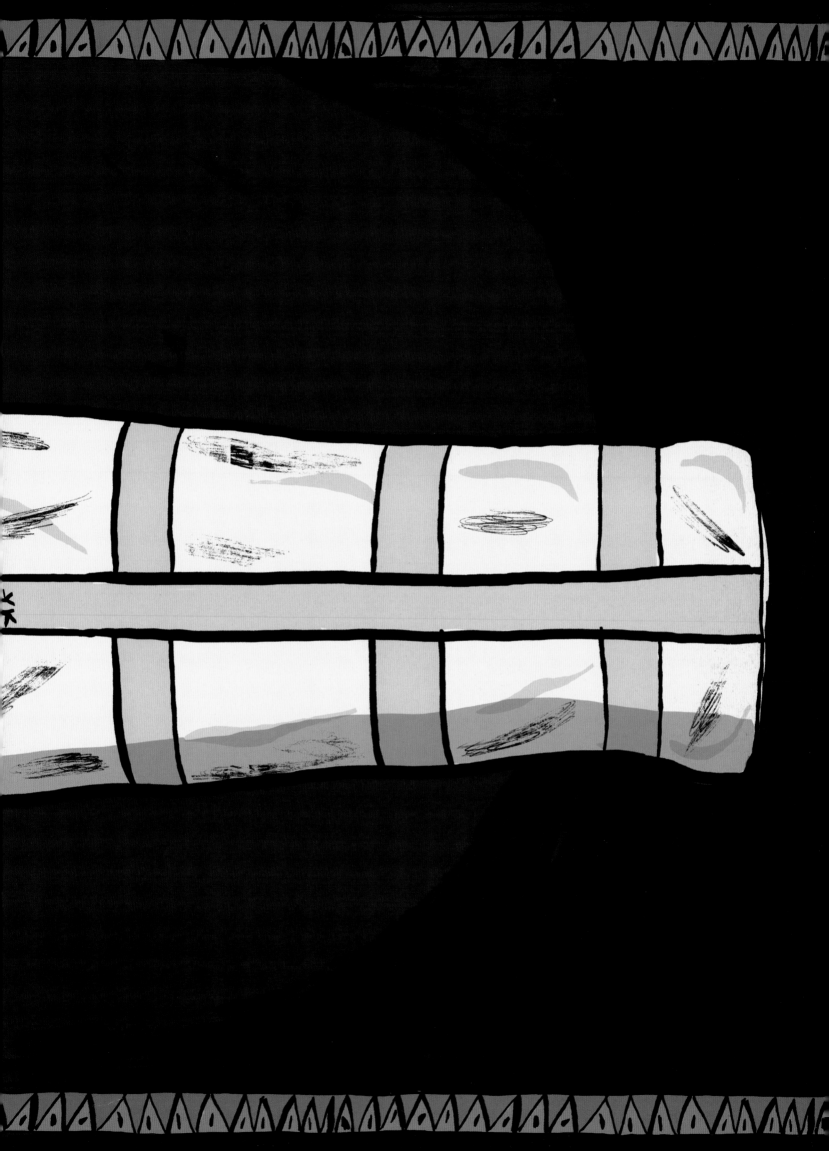

As the wrappings were removed hundreds of amulets (protective charms) and other pieces of jewellery, including seventeen collars, were found between the shrouds. When the body was finally revealed, it was still stuck with the resin. At last Carter and his team were gazing at the corpse of the pharaoh. They were the first people to do so for over 3,000 years.

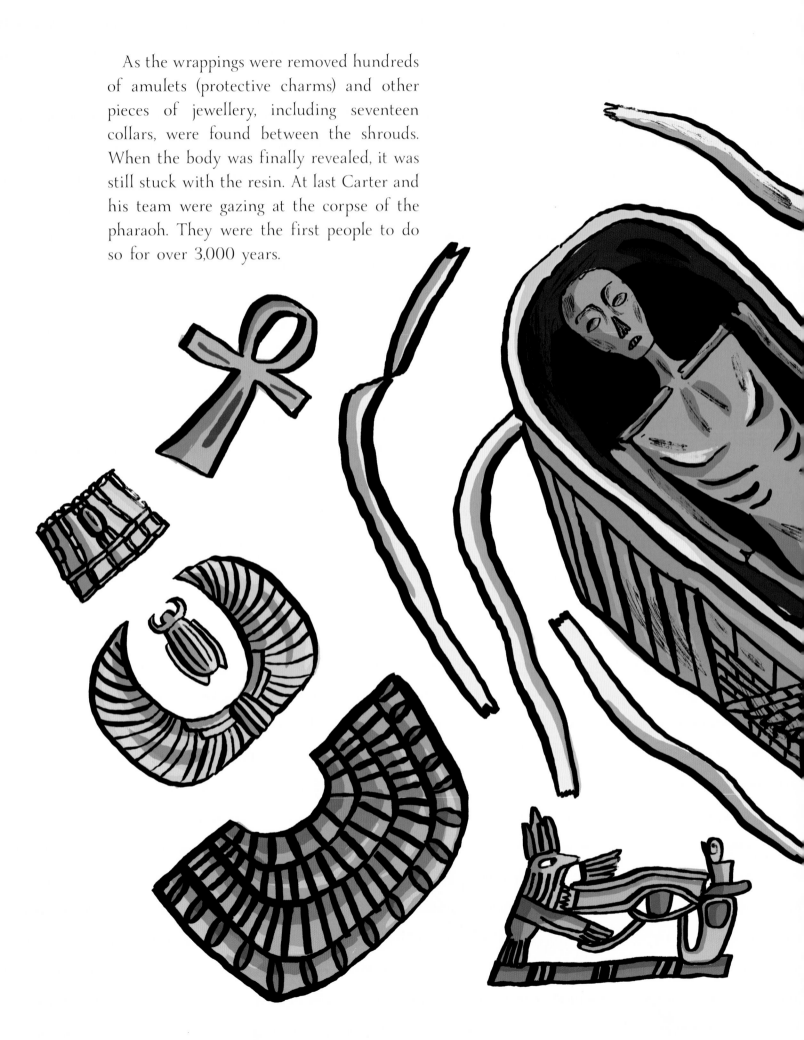

Carter was disappointed to find that the first examinations of Tutankhamun's mummy were unable to confirm a cause of death. They simply revealed that Tutankhamun was a slightly-built youth of about 18 years of age. Later, in 1968, a series of x-rays showed there was a small piece of bone within the skull, possibly from a blow to the head.

THE LAST CHAMBER

The next chamber, the Treasury, held what Carter called "the greatest treasures of the tomb". There was a beautiful gilded shrine, within which Carter found a canopic chest containing the embalmed internal organs: the liver, lungs, intestines and stomach which had been removed from Tutankhamun's body at the time of mummification. A statue of a goddess guarded each side of the shrine. Each goddess faced inwards, with her arms outstretched.

CANOPIC CHEST

It was in the Treasury that Carter also found the most moving objects of all – two miniature coffins containing two tiny, mummified, stillborn baby girls. Carter wondered whether these might have been the daughters of Tutankhamun and Ankhesenamun, however technology was not advanced enough at the time to reveal this.

There was one remaining chamber left to investigate, the Annexe. Carter had noticed it when he first entered the Antechamber but it was five years before he got round to clearing it. This was a difficult task. The clutter it contained was piled so high that workers had to hang from ropes to start clearing the chamber. Carter found it very unusual that these things had been put in the chamber in such a jumble.

There were pieces of pottery, wine jars, and vessels containing oil and lotions, baskets of fruit, stools, games, tables and beds. There were also a large number of shabti figures. Shabtis were little carved statuettes which were buried with people to act as their servants in the afterlife. Usually one or two were buried but 413 were found in Tutankhamun's tomb: that's one servant for each day of the year, plus 36 overseers and 12 directors of different colours.

However, not all of the shabtis bore Tutankhamun's name. This confirmed Carter's suspicion that the shabtis, like the mask on one of the coffins, had been made for the funeral of someone else. This, together with the broken sarcophagus lid, and the hurry with which the king seemed to have been buried, could suggest that this tomb was not intended for Tutankhamun. It was a private rather than a royal tomb. Who the chamber was built for, and why the young pharaoh was buried there instead, Carter did not know.

413 SHABTIS WERE FOUND IN THE TOMB.

Tutankhamun's tomb is the only tomb ever to have been found with the mummy intact, along with so many objects. This makes his tomb the greatest treasure ever discovered, and also the most historically interesting. As well as the valuable jewels and items made from gold, alabaster and precious stones, the tomb contained moving, personal mementoes of the boy king. It is these delicate pieces of clothing, food, toys and family mementoes, which help us to piece together Tutankhamun's life.

Belts, caps, gloves, shirts and over 100 loin cloths.

Two boxes of clothing containing some 50 garments suitable for a little boy and another box labelled "equipment for His Majesty".

A lock of his beloved grandmother Tiye's auburn hair enclosed in a tiny gold coffin.

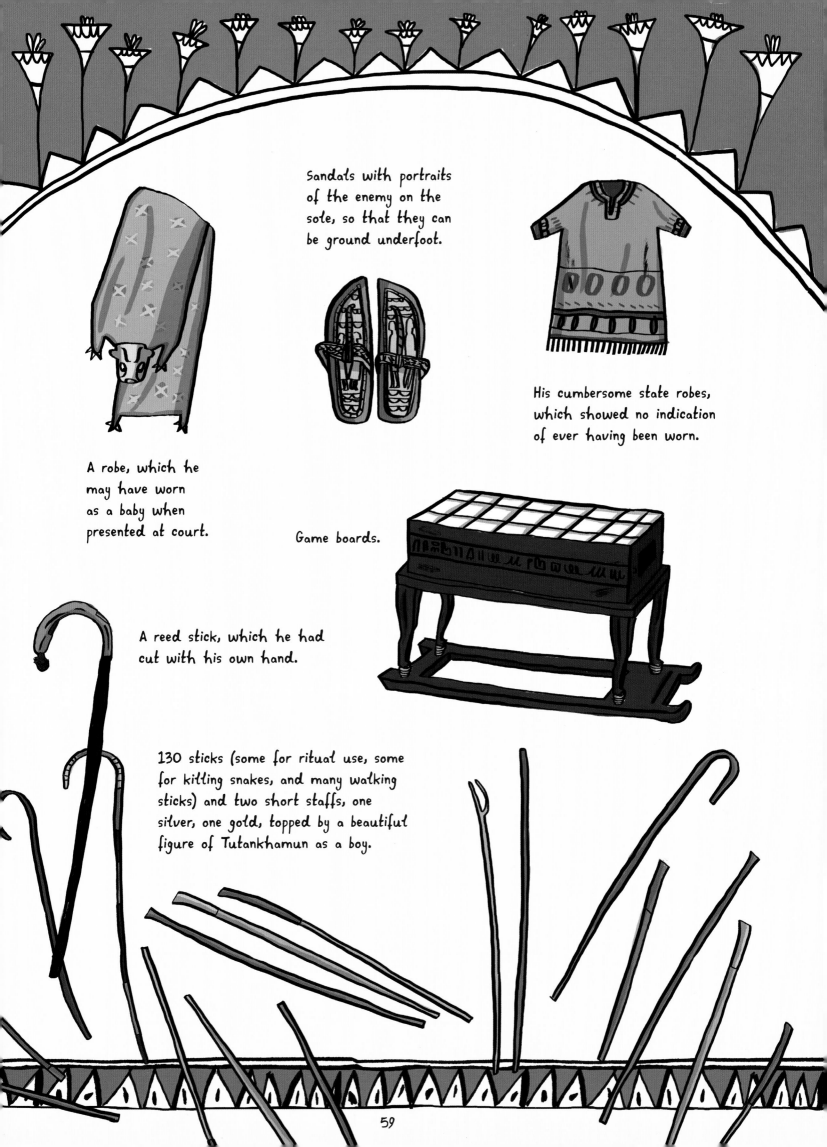

Sandals with portraits of the enemy on the sole, so that they can be ground underfoot.

His cumbersome state robes, which showed no indication of ever having been worn.

A robe, which he may have worn as a baby when presented at court.

Game boards.

A reed stick, which he had cut with his own hand.

130 sticks (some for ritual use, some for killing snakes, and many walking sticks) and two short staffs, one silver, one gold, topped by a beautiful figure of Tutankhamun as a boy.

One of the most interesting items in the tomb was a beautiful chair known as 'The Golden Throne'. Found in the Antechamber, it is made of wood overlaid with sheet gold and silver, and detailed with coloured stones. On the backrest is an exquisite picture of Ankhesenamun and Tutankhamun. They are standing in a floral pavilion and are bathed by the rays of Aten – the sun disc god. This picture bears both aten and amun name-endings, which could mean that Tutankhamun did not completely outlaw his father's Aten cult. Even his corpse wore a beaded skullcap with Tutankhaten written on it.

PART THREE

Mysteries solved, mysteries found

Since Carter's day vast strides have been made in the studies of forensic archaeology and genetics, which have helped to solve some of the mysteries surrounding Tutankhamun's death. Over the years there have been many investigations, and many answers.

A CT scan revealed that Tutankhamun had not been murdered, nor had he died from a blow to the head. The bone found inside his skull had been broken during mummification. A later investigation showed that he had a partial cleft palate, and a bone disease which had destroyed the bone of one of his toes and part of his foot. He also had an unhealed break to his leg and a club foot. This meant he would have found it difficult to walk, so he must have needed a walking stick to move about, which explains why so many walking sticks were found in his tomb. Although these bone conditions would have been very painful they would not have killed him, but they could have weakened him so that he became ill with a strain of malaria. This is a current theory, but we may never know for certain the cause of Tutankhamun's death.

Tests on the two tiny corpses revealed that they were almost certainly the daughters of Tutankhamun and Ankhesenamun. X-rays showed that they both share Tutankhamun's unusual skull shape. We also know from DNA tests that his mother was a sister of his father, Akhenaten.

Some mysteries remain unsolved. We don't know the name of Tutankhamun's mother. Nor do we know what happened to either Nefertiti or Ankhesenamun.

Tutankhamun was buried hurriedly in a tomb built for someone else. Ironically, it is because his tomb was so thoroughly hidden and forgotten, that Tutankhamun's name has been preserved! Perhaps his hurried burial was to hide his death for as long as possible. But why, and from whom, remain unclear.

It can't have been Ay, as he officiated at the burial. However, it may have been his idea to hide the death from Horemheb, to give Ay time to be crowned pharaoh. Although Horemheb was a commoner, he also wanted to become pharaoh, which he eventually did (after the death of Ay). Perhaps the strongest evidence against Horemheb is that when he did become

pharaoh he started destroying everything to do with Tutankhamun's reign and family. Archaeologists have found evidence that inscriptions and names were chiselled away and new names substituted in many cases.

It is possible that Horemheb was away with the army at the time of Tutankhamun's death (perhaps fighting the Hittites, who ruled a powerful empire and were great rivals with the ancient Egyptians). This would have given Ay time to bury Tutankhamun and quickly claim the title of pharaoh for himself (even though officially no king could be crowned until his predecessor was sealed in his tomb). Perhaps he did this to protect the royal family. He married Nefertiti's wet nurse, so after all, he was a part of the royal family. This could account for the rush, but no one knows for certain.

My husband is dead.

Although historians and archaeologists have managed to answer many questions, there remains one more mystery. In the archives of the Hittite kings there are two puzzling letters, which could possibly have come from Ankhesenamun, Tutankhamun's grieving widow. The first says, "My husband is dead I have no son. They say you have many sons. Send me one and I'll make him my husband." This was a very strange request because the two nations were at war, so the Hittite king sent men to investigate. The widow then wrote a second time, "Would I have written to you if I had a son I could marry? My husband is dead and I will not marry a commoner. Send me one of your sons and I will make him king."

I will send you a son.

A son was finally sent, but was ambushed and killed on the way. We can't be sure if Ankhesenamun wrote these letters or not. If she did, it may have been because she was about to be forced into a marriage with someone, perhaps a commoner, she didn't like. It could have been Ay (even though he was much older than her). It is possible that this marriage did take place, but as Ay was royal and not a commoner, it doesn't seems likely. Perhaps it was Horemheb that she was supposed to marry. One theory is that he may have intercepted her letters and had the Hittite prince killed. The mysteries continue.

What became of Howard Carter? Although the discovery made him a household name, he died at the age of 64, isolated and lonely. After completing the excavation of the tomb he retired from archaeology and became an agent for collectors and museums. He sometimes returned to the Winter Palace Hotel in Luxor, the scene of his world-changing discovery. He is buried in London and his epitaphs read:

'O night, spread thy wings
over me as the imperishable stars.'

'May your spirit live,
may you spend millions of years,
you who love Thebes,
sitting with your face to the north wind,
your eyes beholding happiness.'

The last quote is taken from the Lotus Chalice which Carter found in Tutankhamun's tomb, where he had undoubtedly spent the happiest years of his life.

ANNEX

BURIAL CHAMBER

ANTECHAMBER

TREASURY

TUTANKHAMUN'S TOMB